The Middle East

The Changing Strategic Environment

F. Stephen Larrabee

Prepared for the Center for Middle East Public Policy and the
Geneva Centre for Security Policy

RAND NATIONAL SECURITY RESEARCH DIVISION

The conference proceedings described in this report were supported by the RAND Center for Middle East Public Policy and the Geneva Centre for Security Policy.

ISBN 0-8330-3950-4

The RAND Corporation is a nonprofit research organization providing objective analysis and effective solutions that address the challenges facing the public and private sectors around the world. RAND's publications do not necessarily reflect the opinions of its research clients and sponsors.

RAND® is a registered trademark.

Published 2006 by the RAND Corporation
1776 Main Street, P.O. Box 2138, Santa Monica, CA 90407-2138
1200 South Hayes Street, Arlington, VA 22202-5050
4570 Fifth Avenue, Suite 600, Pittsburgh, PA 15213
RAND URL: http://www.rand.org/
To order RAND documents or to obtain additional information, contact
Distribution Services: Telephone: (310) 451-7002;
Fax: (310) 451-6915; Email: order@rand.org

PREFACE

On June 26–28, the Geneva Centre for Security Policy (GCSP) and the Center for Middle East Public Policy (CMEPP) at the RAND Corporation held their sixth annual conference in Gstaad, Switzerland. The conference was devoted to a dialogue on "The Middle East: Changing Strategic Environment." This report summarizes the main issues discussed at the conference.

The RAND Center for Middle East Public Policy is part of International Programs at the RAND Corporation, which aims to improve public policy by providing decisionmakers and the public with rigorous, objective research on critical policy issues affecting the Middle East.

For more information on the RAND Center for Middle East Public Policy, contact the Director, David Aaron. He can be reached by e-mail at David_Aaron@rand.org; by phone at 310-393-0411, extension 7782; or by mail at RAND, 1776 Main Street, Santa Monica, California 90407-2138. More information about RAND is available at www.rand.org.

The Middle East: The Changing Strategic Environment

F. Stephen Larrabee

GCSP/RAND Annual Conference
Gstaad, June 26–28, 2005

On June 26–28, the Geneva Centre for Security Policy (GCSP) and the Center for Middle East Public Policy (CMEPP) at the RAND Corporation held their sixth annual conference in Gstaad, Switzerland. The conference was devoted to a dialogue on "The Middle East: Changing Strategic Environment." This report summarizes the main issues discussed at the conference.

The Peace Process, Democracy, and Stability

The opening session of the conference was devoted to a discussion of democracy and stability in Syria, Jordan, Lebanon, Turkey, Palestine, and Israel.

Jordan. Jordan is facing a double transition: from war to peace and from autocracy to partial democracy. The new prime minister is an academic, but the real power behind the throne is the foreign minister. More Palestinians, it was noted, are moving into positions of power. This is leading to an intensification of the struggle for power between Jordanians and Palestinians. The king wants to give the impression of change. He continues to hold absolute power but is willing to consult more.

Jordan faces several challenges. Economically, the country is dependent on outside aid. The spoils system is growing and becoming harder to manage. Politically, liberalization has run aground. In foreign affairs, U.S. policy poses a challenge. The king is worried that the United States is trying to push Jordan too far, too fast. He also fears the knock-on effect of developments in Lebanon.

Several issues, it was suggested, are likely to be critical in the future:

- How should the economy be reformed?
- How much power is the monarchy willing to cede?
- How can Jordan accommodate U.S. pressures for change?
- What role will the Palestinians have?
- Can Jordan reconcile with Iraq?

The crisis in the past few months has raised serious questions about the king's leadership. The king's brother, the crown prince, is an attractive alternative candidate for the throne. If the current crisis intensifies, the succession issue could reemerge.

Lebanon/Syria. Lebanon also faces important pressures for change. But where these pressures will lead is unclear. It is possible that they could lead to something new. But they could also lead to a new form of foreign domination. The Syrian effort to extend Lahoud's mandate has been the catalyst for a spontaneous challenge to Syrian dominance. The challenge was sparked by popular discontent at the grassroots level and reflected a desire for transparency, less corruption, and a longing for a better standard of living.

In many ways, the political deck is being reshuffled. The power of the Security Services is being challenged. The power of old players is diminishing, and new actors are entering the political arena. As a result, new configurations of power are emerging. But it is unclear what many of these groups really want. The desire for change is strong, but whether the opposition can organize a cohesive reform movement is an open question.

Hezbollah is also undergoing change. It realizes that it has to move from being an armed resistance movement in the South to a political movement reflecting the Shiites. But it wants to avoid the impression that it is changing under U.S. pressure. Hezbollah is not seen by most Lebanese as a radical movement. In Lebanon, it has a positive image and is respected for getting Israel out of Lebanon.

As for Syria, it realizes that a big crunch is coming and that it has to change. Syria will become a net importer of oil in five years. However, the quality of the Syrian leadership is very low. Basher Assad lacks his father's drive and leadership skills, although he is beginning to put non-Baathists and some of his own people in place.

Syrians are also beginning to challenge their leaders and the Security Services. This is an important change. Syria will open up, which will have an inevitable impact on Lebanon.

Turkey. Turkey, it was argued, faces a period of increasing difficulty, both internally and externally. The period since the December 17 decision by the EU to open accession negotiations with Ankara has been characterized by increasing drift. Three issues in particular are cause for concern.

First, relations with the EU have been complicated by the slowdown in reform. Turkey's AKP government seems to be drifting and unsure how to proceed in the wake of the December 17 decision to open accession negotiations. Relations with the EU have been further complicated by the French and Dutch rejection of the EU constitution. The French and Dutch votes made clear that there is considerable popular discontent with the process of enlargement. Moreover, Germany's CDU/CSU party—which is opposed to Turkish membership in the EU—seems likely to win the September 2005 elections. As a result, Turkish chances of joining the EU—already uncertain prior to the French and Dutch votes—now seem even less certain.

Second, relations with the United States remain strained since the March 1, 2003, parliamentary vote rejecting the U.S. request to use Turkish territory to open a second front against Iraq. Relations have been complicated by differences over Iraq, especially the increasing "Kurdization" of Kirkuk, and the refusal of the United States to play a more active military role in combating the Kurdistan Workers Party, which continues to make cross-border attacks on Turkish territory from sanctuaries in Northern Iraq. These differences have been given added impetus by the U.S. effort to portray Turkey as a "model" for the Islamic countries in the Middle East. Many members of the Turkish elite, especially the military, have strong misgivings about such an effort, fearing that it could strengthen Islamic forces in Turkey and weaken Turkey's ties to the West.

Third, there has been a perceptible rise in nationalism in Turkey over the past few years. This has been dramatized in particular by the strong public reaction to the burning of the Turkish flag by several youths in the spring of 2005. Some suggested that the rise of nationalism reflects a growing sense of isolation and insecurity in Turkey, which was worrying to many Western officials.

There was no clear consensus among participants, however, on how serious the problems are. One view held that the situation today is not as bad as it was during the late 1960s and early 1970s, when Turkey had faced significant domestic unrest. This view was contested by one participant, who argued that U.S.-Turkish relations are more seriously strained than many assume. He pointed in particular to a speech in April 2005 by the Chief of the Turkish General Staff General Hilmi Ozkok in which Ozkok openly criticized American policy. Such open criticism is unusual and reflects the growing disenchantment of the military—normally the most pro-American force in Turkey—with U.S. policy, particularly toward Iraq. He also noted that there has been a disturbing growth of anti-Americanism among the Turkish public.

These differences, however, appeared to be more differences of degree rather than major substantive disagreements. On the whole, participants agreed that Turkey's relations with the United States and the EU—especially the latter—are likely to remain strained and that developments in Turkey deserve close monitoring.

Palestine/Israel. Palestinian-Israeli relations seem to be entering a new, somewhat uncertain phase. An important shift has taken place within the Palestinian community. For years there had been a consensus within the Palestinian community that a negotiated settlement was possible. This assumption, it was suggested, is now under challenge. There has been a movement away from an emphasis on a comprehensive solution toward a partial solution. The "Roadmap" had been based on the premise that the hard issues should be negotiated after Palestinian statehood was achieved. Now the comprehensive approach has been disaggregated. Palestinian statehood has been pulled out of the comprehensive approach.

Moreover, the Palestinian Authority seems to be collapsing. Whatever his faults, Arafat had been able to hold everything together. Abu Mazan was elected on a law and order platform, but he is widely perceived as having failed to provide law and order. Cooperation between Fatah and Hamas has deteriorated. In fact, Abu Mazan can point to few successes in his first hundred days. The Gaza withdrawal is regarded by most Palestinians as having more disadvantages than advantages. It reflects Sharon's belief that a negotiated settlement is unattainable and/or undesirable and that the Palestinian side is unable to deliver. Sharon has also moved away from a two-state solution.

Under these circumstances, it was argued, there appear to be four options:

- Parallel unilateralism
- A shift from emphasis on national rights to civic rights
- A new territorial configuration
- A return to Intifada.

On the Israeli side, Sharon, it was argued, has been largely successful in overcoming opposition to disengagement. However, there are several open issues:

- How fast will the withdrawal be?
- What will be the level of cooperation between Israel and Palestine during the withdrawal?
- Will the withdrawal lead to violence?

Early elections in Israel seem likely. Sharon, it was suggested, will probably move to the right. He will not want to pursue negotiations after withdrawing from Gaza. However, the Israeli political system has begun to manifest important structural weaknesses, which are becoming increasingly evident. The electoral system does not really function. As a result, public dissatisfaction with the electoral system is growing. But there is no real interest in changing the system because it would hurt entrenched interests. The economy is growing, but the fruits of this prosperity are not really shared by the majority of the population.

One of the problems is that there is no unified view on what would constitute a two-state solution. The concept means different things to different people. During the conference, the role of outside powers received considerable attention. However, there was no clear consensus among the participants as to what role outside powers can or should play. Several participants argued that the United States should become more actively engaged in the peace process. However, many doubted that this would happen. Others suggested that there was little that outside powers can do because the conditions for a settlement do not exist unless the United States leans heavily on Israel—which few thought was likely to happen.

Several participants lamented the lack of an active role by the Arab states. The Saudi initiative had seemed to suggest that the Arab world was ready to play a more active role in the search for peace. But the initiative has largely become a dead letter. The Arab world, one participant noted, is now under stress and is not open to new ideas at the moment.

Iraq

The situation in Iraq was a major focal point of discussion at the workshop. There was a general consensus that despite American efforts to date to create stability, Iraq lacks a strong and stable government that is capable of providing security. State authority, one participant argued, is collapsing and being replaced by localism. The government in Baghdad has problems extending its power much beyond the Green Zone. The security situation, however, differs in various parts of the country. The Kurdish area in the North is quite stable. The most unstable area is the Sunni Triangle.

The security situation has deteriorated over the last few months. There had been a decline in violence in March and April, but since then the insurgents had regrouped. However, the insurgent movement is not a tightly knit organization with a hierarchal structure. It is composed of three groups: former Baathists and supporters of Sadaam; foreign Jihadists; and criminals. These groups are only loosely connected with no unified core, making the insurgency difficult to defeat.

There was a strong sense among participants that the US policy of "Iraqization" is not working. The most effective Iraqi force is the army, but the police are not very capable. The problem with the police, one participant noted, is not a lack of personnel, but their lack of effectiveness. Another participant argued that it will take at least five years before the Iraqis will be capable of providing for their own security without American assistance.

Few participants, however, believed that the United States would be willing to keep over 100,000 troops in Iraq that long. The tide of U.S. public opinion has begun to turn against the war. Even some members of Bush's own party are beginning to call for a gradual withdrawal of U.S. troops. The pressures for a phased withdrawal, one participant argued, are likely to grow over the next year, forcing the administration to begin withdrawing some troops. He cited five sources of pressure for a phased withdrawal:

- The possibility of a new crisis (Iran, North Korea) which requires the United States to focus its attention away from Iraq
- Growing economic pressures as a result of rising oil prices
- Rising discontent within the Republican party as the midterm elections approach
- The possibility of a "Tet Offensive–like" event that catches the United States by surprise and has a devastating political-psychological effect on the U.S. public
- Rising discontent within the U.S. military about the effects of over-extension on the military's ability to carry out other missions.

Taken together, these developments, he argued, would force the Bush administration to begin to draw down U.S. forces before the midterm elections.

There was strong feeling among many participants that there are no good short-term options and that it will be difficult to turn the situation in Iraq around. As one participant noted, the insurgents do not have to defeat the United States; they "just have to not lose to win." Solutions that might have worked at one point had been rejected. By the time they were resurrected, it was too late. The internal dynamics have changed.

The Europeans, one European participant noted, are divided. On the one hand, many are happy that the United States is bogged down in Iraq; this allows Europe to portray itself as the "good guy" in the Middle East. On the other hand, they do not want the United States to withdraw precipitously because this could have a destabilizing impact not only on Iraq but on the whole Middle East.

There was a strong sense among participants that Iran will be an important player in the future. U.S. policy, however, largely leaves Iran out of the equation. This is a mistake, several participants argued, because Iran will end up playing the role of a spoiler.

Iran's Nuclear Program

Iran's nuclear policy was also a central theme at the workshop. Europe's role in trying to prevent Iran from acquiring nuclear weapons received particular attention. European involvement was seen as motivated by several factors:

- The desire to overcome the divisions precipitated by the Iraq crisis
- The desire to play a more prominent role in preventing nuclear proliferation
- The development of an Iranian ballistic missile program
- The strategic consequences for the Middle East of an Iranian nuclear bomb
- The impact of an Iranian nuclear bomb on the nuclear Non-Proliferation Treaty (NPT) regime.

In the discussions between the European troika (France, Germany and Great Britain) and Iran, two agreements had been reached. The first was in October 2003; the second was in November 2004. Both agreements targeted the suspension of the fuel cycle, but the second was more precise and comprehensive. The first agreement, which collapsed in June 2004, opened a long discussion about the perimeter of the suspension. The second agreement banned not only any conversion, enrichment, and reprocessing but also any assembling and testing of centrifuges.

Economically, one European participant pointed out, Iran's fuel cycle activities make no sense (since there is only one reactor, built by Russia, with fuel provided for 10 years), but militarily they make great sense. Moreover, Iran has been engaged in a policy of concealment and obfuscation for roughly 20 years. Past Iranian concealment has included acquisitions (nuclear materials and equipment), sites (Kalaye, Natanz, Arak, Lashkar Abad, Lavizan-Shian, Parchin), and activities (conversion into uranium metal, production of beryllium and polonium). In February 2003, the IAEA demanded full access to the Kalaye Electric facility, but it was not granted until August 2003. When inspectors were finally admitted to the site, major refurbishing was noted. Inspections were constantly delayed (Lavizan-Shian), explanations shifted with discoveries (on the P2 centrifuges, for instance), and access to key facilities was refused (Parchin).

Consistent with the NPT, the European view is that Article 4, which permits peaceful uses, is conditional on Iran's commitment to remain a nonnuclear state. The Russian reactor and access to Russian fuel guarantees Iran peaceful nuclear energy use. Peaceful use is thus not much of an issue. At this point, one conference participant suggested, there are really three key issues:

- *The origin of the low grade and highly enriched uranium found in Iran.* After having declared that all equipment was indigenous, Iran claimed that highly enriched uranium identified by inspectors at different sites was the result of contamination from foreign components. This point is almost impossible to verify in a satisfactory manner because Pakistan does not provide access to its territory and the exact origin of pieces brought by Pakistani experts to Vienna is impossible to determine with certainty.
- *P-2 centrifuge activities between 1995 and 2002.* The International Atomic Energy Agency (IAEA) does not believe the Iranian story concerning the complete lack of activity during this period, after the acquisition of the P-2 designs from the A.Q. Khan network.
- *The exact nature of the 1987 Pakistani offer.* Since the IAEA has only a partial copy of the offer, there is some possibility that it included weapons design, as was the case in Libya.

However, despite Iranian efforts at concealment and obfuscation, there have been some positive developments in the last two years. European, U.S., and Russian coordination and cooperation have improved, and revelations about Iranian activities continue to leak out. But in the wake of the presidential elections, it is not clear how the Iranians will proceed.

If the agreement were to be violated, one European participant insisted, the Europeans would be prepared to bring the issue before the UN Security Council. Others, however, questioned the concrete meaning of this declaration. As one American participant framed it: "And then what?" Others felt that much will depend on the nature of the new regime in Tehran. This leadership, they argued, is inexperienced and unlikely to understand the exact nature of what they face. Domestic factors will also be important. The new regime will need to be able to sell any policy domestically. Freezing nuclear activities, it was argued, is one thing; dismantlement is quite another.

Iran's nuclear ambitions raise three critical problems. The first is the potential acquisition of the bomb by a new nation in the Middle East and the consequences this development would prompt. Another is the transfer problem (including, again, not only the activities of the A.Q. Khan network, but also the role of Russia, China, and North Korea in the Iranian program). The third is the problem of leakage. One participant argued that this is the most serious concern, an opinion that seemed debatable to others. It is easier, he argued, for terrorists to acquire nuclear technology via leakage than through the deliberate government transfer of technology.

The Iranian leadership views its involvement in Iraq as a useful bargaining chip. If the West would agree to reduce its pressure on the nuclear issue, Iran has suggested it could be helpful in Iraq. As one participant argued, Iran wants to see the United States bogged down in Iraq, but it does not want the United States to win quickly enough to free forces for use against Iran.

It was noted that countries in the region have not made a major public issue out of Iran's nuclear ambitions, despite the effect that Iran's acquisition of nuclear weapons would have on the entire Middle East. One reason, it was suggested, is that the countries in the region do not want to deflect critical attention away from Israel's nuclear program. Another is that U.S. prestige is so low that none of the countries in the region want to be seen siding with the United States.

The Iranian acquisition of nuclear weapons, however, would have grave strategic implications for the region. Geographically, the Gulf states are close to Iran, and several have U.S. forces deployed within their territory. In the event of U.S. military action against Iran, it is feared that Iran might retaliate against those states in the region closely allied with the United States. In addition, several participants noted, Iran's acquisition of nuclear weapons could stimulate other states in the region, especially Egypt and Saudi Arabia, to seek a nuclear option.

Russia's role was also discussed. Russia, one participant argued, is tired of Iranian cheating. At the same time, it considers Iran a strategic partner in the region and part of a "Rising Asia," which also includes India and China. It is also unclear whether all the past Russian deals with Iran have already surfaced. But another participant pointed out that Russia's position has evolved. In the 1990s, Russia had been a major proliferator. Today, Moscow says it would take Iran before the UN Security Council. Others, however, doubted whether Russia would really do this. Both China and Russia, it was pointed out, have shielded Iran at the NPT conference. The reality test will come if and when the dossier is submitted to the UN in New York.

The U.S. policy toward Iran, several participants suggested, does not seem clear or consistent. The Bush administration appears divided on how to deal with Iran. Some in the administration seem to favor a policy of regime change and believe that military action would cause the collapse of the regime; others believe that military action would solidify support for the regime. Moreover, U.S.-European solidarity appears fragile.

Several participants questioned whether a serious military option did in fact exist. Iran's nuclear facilities, they pointed out, are hardened and dispersed; some are reportedly in densely populated areas. Others argued that a military option did exist, but the problem would be the political costs. A military strike against Iran, they insisted, would solidify support for the regime, increase anti-American sentiment within the Iranian population, and risk retaliation against U.S. allies in the region.

The US, the EU, and UN Security Council

The discussion in this session centered on three principal issues: the prospects for stability and change in the Middle East, NATO's future role, and the role of multilateral institutions in enhancing security and stability.

Addressing the American role and perspective on the Middle East, one American speaker noted that the United States will be preoccupied with the Middle East for at least the next decade. While 11/9 (the fall of the Berlin wall) had marked the end of the cold War, 9/11 (the attacks on the Twin Towers and the Pentagon) signaled the end of American invulnerability. It also accelerated the debate on the democratization of the Middle East. The United States and Europe, he argued, have no choice but to engage in the Middle East. The Europeans have a responsibility to help the United States stabilize the region. At the same time, the United States lacks a grand strategy for the Middle East. However, the United States, he suggested, is beginning to realize that it needs allies.

NATO, it was argued, faces a new agenda. During the Cold War, Europe had been the focal point of NATO's agenda. Today, this agenda is focused on security problems beyond Europe's border. Europe and the United States share common interests in dealing with this new agenda. The Solana document (European Security Strategy) demonstrated that U.S. and European perspectives on the main threats are remarkably similar. Europe, one participant maintained, should help the United States restructure NATO to carry out this new agenda. In addition, the United States and Europe need to develop a joint U.S.-European grand strategy for the Middle East.

Elaborating on these themes, another American addressed the prospects for collective action. The Iraq debate, he argued, has really been a debate about American power. In the 1990s, there had been no effort to try to balance American power because American power was embedded in multilateral institutions. This had changed in the 2000s. The Bush administration had shifted to a unilateralist course. This prompted an effort by Chirac, Schroeder, and Putin to try to balance U.S. power.

The Bush administration also adopted a different approach to the question of sovereignty. It had put greater emphasis on regime change. It had also made preemption a principle of U.S. national strategy. Today, he suggested, there are two main tensions in U.S. policy:

- A tension between working with multilateral institutions or outside of them
- A tension between regime change and behavior change.

While most participants agreed that the United States and Europe needed each other, U.S. and European perceptions, many argued, are not identical. In the Middle East, the United States puts great emphasis on Israel, combating terrorism, and promoting democracy. The Europeans, by contrast, focus more on stability and see instability as the main threat in the region. Europe, one European participant argued, is still interested in NATO. The real question, he suggested, is whether the United States is still interested in NATO. The U.S. emphasis on coalitions of the willing seems to suggest that the United States is downgrading NATO as an instrument of U.S. security.

Europe, it was argued, will be able to carry out peacekeeping but lacks the capability to conduct major combat missions. The main weaknesses are in the areas of transport, precision guided munitions, and reconnaissance. Less than one-third of the available brigades are capable of being deployed abroad. Most European participants felt, however, that the French and Dutch votes will not have a major impact on European Security and Defense Policy (ESDP). The French and Dutch votes represent discontent with enlargement, immigration, and unemployment, not ESDP, which enjoys strong support among European publics. There might be some slight loss of momentum, they suggested, but it is unlikely this will have a major impact on ESDP.

The Middle East proved to be the most contentious issue. While one American argued the need for greater Western assistance to the Middle East, several of the Middle Eastern participants cautioned against such a policy, arguing that it would do little good and that the money would just be wasted or spent on buying more weapons. They advocated a case-by-case approach. Others questioned whether the United States would really allow free elections. If it did, the Islamic forces would be likely to emerge victorious in many cases. Several suggested that the West should stop subsidizing the Security Services. Instead, they argued, Washington should support programs that strengthened civil society in the Middle East.

The United States cannot have it both ways, one participant argued. The genie is out of the bottle. The United States will be judged by its rhetoric. But there will be a price to pay. The United States has made democracy promotion a key tenet of its Middle East policy. Now, he asserted, it will be expected to live up to its rhetoric.

As for Europe, a European participant suggested that Europe would be better off emphasizing rule of law rather than democracy. Another participant suggested that the West should heed the lessons of the French experience in Algeria. France had made a mistake when it thwarted the electoral process. This led to an upswing of terrorism on French soil.

Countering Islamic Terrorism

The workshop devoted considerable attention to the issue of countering Islamic terrorism. A strategy to counter Islamic terrorism, one participant suggested, will require four elements: interdict, confront/defeat, delegitimize, and address root causes. Progress is being made on the first two elements; the fourth is long-term. The third area (delegitimize) is where the West is weakest and where opportunities are being missed.

Radical Muslim groups in Europe are emerging as a particular problem. There are some 12 million Muslims in Western Europe. German security services list 31,800 members of 24 radical Islamist groups, not including jihadists, the number of which they refuse to estimate. One of the most important factors contributing to the radicalization of Muslims in Europe is the failure of these groups to assimilate. There is a growing underclass, which is poorly educated, has few employment opportunities, and feels increasingly alienated and disaffected. This community is increasingly susceptible to radicalization. Many of them are not particularly religious; they have a variety of identities.

Even before 9/11, European governments had begun taking steps to deal with the threat posed by Muslim extremists, such as making rules of evidence and prosecution easier. Not all these measures, however, have gone into effect yet. Efforts are also being made to deal with the root causes, but it is not clear that these efforts will be any more effective than previous efforts.

Some European governments are attempting to identify counterparts—that is, selecting groups that are moderate and nonviolent and establishing them as official representatives. It is not clear, however, to what extent these groups are really representative of the Muslim communities in their respective countries.

Some studies have looked at targets of terror attacks to try to assess the goals of the terrorists. Such efforts, however, have not been very effective. Looking at communities from which radicals have emerged and the radicals' personality traits, it was suggested, is more effective. It is also important to identify communities that oppose terrorist acts and seek to co-opt them as allies in countering the threat of Islamic terrorism.

One of the basic problems, another participant argued, is that there is no clarity or consensus on the nature of the threat. Is the threat jihadists, Islamists, or terror in general? Second, there is no systemic conception of the threat—what is driving it and how various elements are related to one another. Finally, there is no comprehensive, integrated strategy to counter the threat. As a result, actions taken are unorganized, unconnected to one another, and short-term.

There is also a problem, he suggested, with terminology. The 9/11 commission had focused on Islamist (not Islamic) terror rather than terror more broadly. The same participant suggested "Islamist militancy" is a more useful term. This includes three groups: transnational/jihadist groups, nationalist/insurgent groups, and support/mobilization groups.

Islamist militancy needs to be embedded in a comprehensive, dynamic framework. The current threat is not a traditional security or terrorist threat. Some see it as a global threat requiring a global counter-insurgency approach. The United States Institute of Peace (USIP) favors instead an epidemiological approach, which focuses on host, agent, environment, and vectors. The counter-epidemic approach seeks to

- counter existing outbreaks
- prevent new outbreaks
- remedy environmental conditions.

For U.S. strategy, this means controlling the most virulent activities, preventing the spread of Islamist militancy among high-risk, high-value targets in the Muslim world, and remedying the contributing conditions in the Muslim world. These actions have to be taken simultaneously not sequentially.

A third participant suggested that terms are important and can be counterproductive. Up until 9/11, the term generally used had been "combating terrorism." This suggested that we were dealing with an enduring task. It had generally focused on law enforcement, but at times had also included military measures.

The focus shifted after 9/11 to doing everything necessary worldwide to dismantle al Qaeda and organizations responsible for the attacks on the Twin Towers and the Pentagon. We now have a global war on terror. This is less focused on al-Qaeda. Such a global war is counterproductive, the participant argued. It is too broad to serve as a useful policy framework.

There has been undeniable progress on the narrower struggle. The Taliban have been removed from power. A number of al Qaeda's key leaders have been killed or captured. Many governments have been galvanized into action. But there have also been many setbacks. Al Qaeda has survived and is continuing to recruit new followers. U.S. actions have provoked the Muslim world and alienated allies. Al Qaeda's financial and communications networks are still intact.

The future, however, does not appear to be particularly bright. Pressures for the United States to withdraw troops from Iraq are likely to grow as the 2008 presidential elections approach. Chaos would likely ensue in Iraq after a U.S. withdrawal, providing new opportunities for the jihadists. Afghanistan could slide back into chaos. Pakistan could face greater turmoil. Instability in Saudi Arabia could increase.

Moreover, the war on terror, it was suggested, has demonstrated that superpowers are vulnerable. Superior conviction can defeat technology. Small unconventional forces can prevail through ambush and bleeding an opponent to death. Casualties are more important to the West than to jihadists. This is an enduring—possibly centuries long—conflict.

In the discussion, several participants pointed to the inadequacy of the terms used in the debate on terrorism. Terrorism, one suggested, is too much of a blanket term. Terrorism is not a unifying factor like communism; it is a tactic. It is important, he cautioned, to set priorities and not to overreact.

There was disagreement among participants about the attitude of the Muslim populations to the use of terrorism. Some participants argued that the vast majority of the

Arab world does not condemn the use of terrorism; some, it was suggested, even secretly applaud it. They prefer Bin Laden and Zarqawi to Bush and Rumsfeld. Bin Laden has been able to tap into decades of pent-up anger, hostility and a sense of humiliation. Others maintained that the vast majority of Muslims in the Middle East are appalled by the destruction of other Muslims.

The effect of the new recruits returning from Iraq was also raised. One participant asked, What will be the impact of these new recruits on the terrorism problem in Europe? How will Europe deal with this problem?

Saudi Arabia/GCC

The final session of the conference was devoted to a discussion of developments in Saudi Arabia and Egypt.

Saudi Arabia. Saudi Arabia, it was argued, is facing increased pressures for reform. These pressures are both internal and external. The internal pressures are stimulated by public expectations of an improvement in the quality of social services, improved educational opportunities, and the fact that the Saudi population is growing faster than the GDP. These pressures are reinforced by a youth bulge. Externally, Saudi Arabia faces growing U.S. pressure for reform. This pressure has increased as a result of the fact that the Bush administration has made democracy promotion a central tenet of its foreign policy. But U.S. pressure for reform is creating important tensions between democracy, security, and stability.

Women's rights are becoming an important social issue in Saudi Arabia. However, most demands are made peacefully, not through violence. A dialogue on women's rights and youth has begun. There have been many recommendations. Few, however, have actually been implemented. Public and private human rights organizations are being created, but they remain carefully controlled by the government. Even officials of private human rights organizations are appointed by the government. Academics need the approval of the Ministry of Education to take part in international conferences.

What is critically needed, one participant argued, is a sustained commitment by the government to reform and a new social contract. The Saudi population wants better management of the country's oil wealth and better social services. Popular dissatisfaction with the quality of social services and public infrastructure is growing. There is also a vital need for more institution-building. The key challenge, it was suggested, will be to find a balance between external pressure for reform, internal pressure for reform, and what the government is willing to do.

Until May 2003, no one in Saudi Arabia had really believed that Saudis were involved in the 9/11 attacks. Since the terrorist attacks in the kingdom in May 2003, however, Saudi s has begun to call for stronger action, and steps have been taken against potential terrorist groups. The royal family's primary goal has been to retain power. They have proven to be quite pragmatic in pursuing this goal, including cracking down on indigenous terrorism.

After 9/11, the clergy convinced the government that they were both in the same boat. They are opposed to liberals and their agenda. Supporters of a constitutional monarchy have been jailed. However, one participant noted, it is important to differentiate between the Saudi nationalists who believed in women's rights, etc., and liberals, who are viewed as pro-U.S. or supporters of the West. The government is trying to balance the two forces, but it has become increasingly difficult to do so.

The clergy has played an important role in the Saudi municipal elections. Their support has made a big difference. However, the significance of the elections, it was argued, should not be overrated: There was really very little power at stake. Moreover, turnout was quite low. Voting was difficult: if someone wanted to vote for seven people, he had to go to seven different places to vote for them.

The role of the Gulf Cooperation Council (GCC) was also discussed. Iraq, it was noted, has provoked a major debate within the GCC. U.S. policy is seen by members as amplifying the threat. Like Britain during the days of the Ottoman empire, the United States has convinced the governments of the region that it is the only solution to the region's problem. At the same time, there is increasing debate within the GCC on a variety of issues, especially the issue of signing bilateral free trade agreements. However, the GCC is reluctant to act as a mediator. It prefers instead to decide internally what to do.

However, one participant noted, there is a growing awareness that the GCC needs to play a more active role. At the same time, several participants argued that the United States needs to reassess its policy in the region and put less emphasis on the military aspects. Instead what is needed, they suggested, is a more inclusive approach—one that included Yemen and Iraq—and the creation of a new security architecture for the region.

NATO, it was argued, could play a role in enhancing Gulf security. The United States could be more effective working through NATO than by acting unilaterally. By working through NATO, it would be seen less as an occupying force. However, NATO's role, it was suggested, should not be limited simply to training Iraqi security forces. NATO could play a useful role in fostering cooperation in areas such as intelligence-sharing and some areas of soft security.

Egypt. To understand what is transpiring in Egypt today, it was argued, it is necessary to see current developments—and the current regime — in historical context. The last serious challenge the regime faced was in the period 1992–1996/7. The current challenge is qualitatively less significant. The previous challenge had proven useful as a scapegoat for the worsening of economic conditions. It had helped generate U.S. support and been useful in building a domestic coalition.

However, the current challenge does not provide similar opportunities. Occasional demonstrations cannot be blamed for Egypt's economic problems. The rationale for the political coalition is also weaker now that the militants have been eliminated. People are annoyed by the current political restrictions and do not accept the need for a united front any longer. The rationale is also less convincing to the United States, which has made democracy promotion a cornerstone of its Middle Eastern policy.

The Muslim Brotherhood presents the most serious challenge today. It is the most organized opposition force and the most organized force in the country. Moreover, it has an internal cohesiveness. By contrast, the government lacks any real ideology. Polls suggest that the Muslim Brotherhood could get up to 25 percent of the vote in a fair and free election. However, this probably underestimates the group's strength, since people tend to lie to pollsters.

The regime is facing a problem of increasing delegitimization. It is confronted with multiple and simultaneous demonstrations. These are not acts of violence but unlicensed demonstrations designed to demonstrate the meaninglessness of the government's regulations. In the past, the regime could argue that it could not cooperate with the opposition. The demonstrations, however, have weakened this argument and have forced the regime to recognize the need to work with the opposition because of the number of people it can mobilize.

Despite the increased unrest, the regime seems unlikely to collapse. Both the road to violence and the road to elections are blocked. However, there is a clear change in the political climate. People are losing their fear and are no longer afraid to speak out. Many are particularly incensed by Mubarak's attempt to groom his son Gemal to succeed him.

At the same time, relations with Washington have deteriorated as a result of the Bush administration's emphasis on democracy promotion. However, many in the regime hope the Pentagon will keep lobbying for them. They think the United States is bluffing and that at heart it favors stability over greater participation. They also believe that 9/11 and the war on terrorism will make the United States more sympathetic toward a crackdown on the Muslim Brotherhood.

Appendix A

THE MIDDLE EAST: CHANGING STRATEGIC ENVIRONMENT
GCSP/RAND ANNUAL CONFERENCE
GSTAAD, 26 – 28 JUNE 2005
Programme

Sunday, 26 June 2005 Arrival of Participants

19h30   **Welcoming Dinner at the Hotel Olden**

Keynote address: The New Strategic Context

Dr. Geoffrey KEMP, Director, Regional Strategic Programs, The Nixon Center, Washington, D.C.

Monday, 27 June 2005 Introduction

09h00-09h30   **Welcome and Introduction to the Conference**

Ambassador David AARON, Director, Center for Middle East Public Policy, RAND

Dr. Shahram CHUBIN, Head of Academic Affairs, GCSP

Dr. James A. THOMSON, President and CEO, RAND Corporation, Santa Monica

09h30-11h30   **Peace Process: Democracy and Stability**

Chair: Dr. Shahram CHUBIN, Head of Academic Affairs, GCSP

Syria / Jordan

Mr. Tariq TELL, Jordan

Dr. Samir ALTAQI, Center for Strategic Studies, Damascus University, Damascus

Lebanon

Dr. Ghassan SALAMÉ, Research Director, Center for International Studies and Research (CERI), Paris

Mr. Rami KHOURI, Editor-at-large, The Daily Star, Beirut

Turkey

Dr. Philip J. ROBINS, Lecturer in the Politics of the Middle East, Oxford University

Palestine

Dr. Ahmad KHALIDI, Senior Associate Member, St. Antony's College, Oxford University

Israel

Brig. Gen. (res.) Shlomo BROM, Senior Research Associate, The Jaffee Center for Strategic Studies, Tel Aviv

11h30-12h00	*Coffee Break*
12h00-13h00	**General Discussion**
13h00-14h00	*Buffet Lunch*

14h00-15h30   Iraq: Stabilisation

Chair: Dr. James A. THOMSON, President and CEO, RAND Corporation, Santa Monica

Dr. Toby DODGE, Queen Mary, University of London and the International Institute for Strategic Studies (IISS), London

Ms. Olga OLIKER, Senior Researcher, RAND, Washington, D.C

15h30-16h00	*Coffee Break*
16h00-17h00	**General Discussion**
19h30	*Dinner at the Restaurant Rialto*

Tuesday, 28 June 2005

09h00-10h30   Iran's Nuclear Programme and the Region

Chair: Dr. Geoffrey KEMP, Director, Regional Strategic Programs, The Nixon Center, Washington, D.C.

Dr. Shahram CHUBIN, Head of Academic Affairs, GCSP

Dr. Thérèse DELPECH, Director of Strategic Affairs, Commissariat à l'Energie Atomique (CEA)

10h30-11h00   *Coffee Break*

11h00-13h00   The US, the EU and the UN Security Council

Chair: Ambassador David AARON, Director, Center for Middle East Public Policy, RAND

Ambassador Robert HUNTER, Senior Advisor, RAND Washington, D.C.

Dr. Robert LITWAK, Director, Division of International Studies, Woodrow Wilson International Center for Scholars, Washington, D.C.

Dr. Stefano SILVESTRI, President, Institute for International Affairs (IAI), Rome

13h00-14h00   *Buffet Lunch*

14h00-15h30   **Countering Islamist Terrorism**

Chair: Mr. Brian JENKINS, Senior Advisor, RAND, Santa Monica

Dr. Paul STARES, Director, Research and Studies Program, United States Institute of Peace (USIP), Washington, D.C.

Dr. Cheryl BENARD, Senior Researcher, RAND, Washington D.C.

15h30-16h00   *Coffee Break*
16h00-17h30   **Saudi Arabia / GCC**

Chair: Dr. Thérèse DELPECH, Director of Strategic Affairs, Commissariat à l'Energie Atomique (CEA)

Dr. Abdulaziz SAGER, Chairman, Gulf Research Centre, Dubai

Dr. Ibrahim KARAWAN, Director, Middle East Center, University of Utah

19h30   *Concluding Informal Dinner* at the Hotel Bellevue

Rapporteur   Dr. F. Stephen LARRABEE, Corporate Chair in European Security, RAND

Appendix B

THE MIDDLE EAST: CHANGING STRATEGIC ENVIRONMENT
GCSP/RAND ANNUAL CONFERENCE
GSTAAD, 26 – 28 JUNE 2005
Participants List

Ambassador David AARON, Director, Center for Middle East Public Policy, RAND, Santa Monica

Ms. Livia Leu AGOSTI, Minister/Deputy Head of Division, Political Division II Africa/Middle East, Federal Department for Foreign Affairs, Bern

Dr. Cheryl BENARD, Senior Researcher, RAND, Washington D.C.

Brig. Gen. (res.) Shlomo BROM, Senior Research Associate, The Jaffee Center for Strategic Studies, Tel Aviv

Dr. Shahram CHUBIN, Head of Academic Affairs, GCSP

Dr. Thérèse DELPECH, Director of Strategic Affairs, Commissariat à l'Energie Atomique (CEA), Paris

Dr. Toby DODGE, Queen Mary, University of London, and the International Institute for Strategic Studies (IISS), London

Mr. Marc FINAUD, Faculty Member, GCSP

Ambassador Robert HUNTER, Senior Advisor, RAND, Washington, D.C.

Mr. Brian JENKINS, Senior Advisor, RAND, Santa Monica

Dr. Ibrahim KARAWAN, Director, Middle East Center, University of Utah, Salt Lake City

Dr. Geoffrey KEMP, Director, Regional Strategic Programs, The Nixon Center, Washington, D.C.

Mr. Rami KHOURI, Editor-at-large, The Daily Star, Beirut

Dr. Ahmad KHALIDI, Senior Associate Member, St. Antony's College, Oxford University

Dr. F. Stephen LARRABEE, Corporate Chair in European Security, RAND, Santa Monica

Dr. Robert LITWAK, Director, Division of International Studies, Woodrow Wilson International Center for Scholars, Washington, D.C.

Dr. Arnold LÜTHOLD, Senior Fellow (Middle East), Geneva Centre for the Democratic Control of Armed Forces (DCAF)

Ms. Olga OLIKER, Senior Researcher, RAND, Washington, D.C.

Dr. Vladimir ORLOV, Faculty Member, GCSP

Dr. Philip J. ROBINS, Lecturer in the Politics of the Middle East, Oxford University

Dr. Abdulaziz SAGER, Chairman, Gulf Research Centre, Dubai

Dr. Stefano SILVESTRI, President, Institute for International Affairs (IAI), Rome

Dr. Paul STARES, Director, Research and Studies Program, United States Institute of Peace (USIP) Washington, D.C.

Dr. Fred TANNER, Deputy Director, GCSP

Mr. Tariq TELL, Amman

Dr. James A. THOMSON, President and CEO, RAND Corporation, Santa Monica